# ACE Notes Guide to achieving an A* with "Of Mice and Men"

"Of Mice and Men" is a longstanding favourite text for G.C.S.E. exams and Controlled Assessments. It's not a long book but it is packed with themes, representative characters, imagery, social comment – the list is endless and this is why the book has proved to be perennially popular with students, teachers and examiners. It is also a rich source of ideas for analysis which can impress examiners and force them to place your work in the highest bands of assessment.

The aim of this revision resource is to give you the tools and ideas to achieve an A grade or preferably an A* grade in responses to the text of "Of Mice and Men". If you are capable of a C grade, you can use some of the following tips and analysis points to manoeuver your exam answers into the very top grades.

As a successful Head of English in a London comprehensive school, the details I will give you have been tried, tested and proved to be highly successful in guiding students to the top for many years. It must be emphasised that there is no magic formula to make you cruise to success with no effort – the aim of this resource is to put you in the position where you can create your own success.

# In this resource you will find:

- Consideration of John Steinbeck's intentions for the book and the effect it would have upon his readers.
- Discussion on why the author created each character - what did each character contribute to the message which the author wanted to put across?
- What is the point of Candy?
- What is the point of Crooks?
- What is the point of Curley?
- What is the point of Curley's Wife?
- What is the point of Slim?
- What is the point of Whit?
- What is the point of the Boss?
- What is the point of the bus driver?
- What is the point of Carlson?
- What is the point of George?
- What is the point of Lennie?
- What is the point of Candy's dog?
- What is the significance of the ranch?
- What is the significance of the horseshoe game?
- What is the significance of the opening scene?
- What is the significance of the closing scene?
- Discussion of the importance of settings to the author's message.
- Suggestions for essay/answer planning
- Model introductions to essays on the novel
- Detailed sample essay plans
- Useful targeted quotes

# The aim of this booklet

The key approach for those students aiming for the higher grades is breadth and depth of analysis. That is to say we don't just comment on the story and its characters but we spend most of our time considering the implications of the story, characters and action.

One of the main interests of examiners over the past few years is the candidates' ability to recognise and comment on author's voice. In other words, they want you to explain and evaluate what message you think the author was trying to put across to his/ her readers. Throughout this booklet, you will be given some ideas on what the author's intentions may have been thereby enabling you to travel along the A* path of analysis.

# Consideration of John Steinbeck's intentions for the book and the effect it would have upon his readers.

As a well known socialist, John Steinbeck was concerned with the lives and wellbeing of ordinary people. He saw many faults in the organisation and ethos of America at the time he was writing "Of Mice and Men" and so it is reasonable to assume he wanted to put forward ideas which could sow the seeds of change in American society. Steinbeck himself had experience of working on the ranches of California so he could add realism and power to his writing simply through being intimately familiar with some of the scenarios and attitudes he was describing. He would also have understood the difficulties and worries which the workers of America were living with every day.

We are all familiar with the saying "the pen is mightier than the sword" and Steinbeck certainly used his pen to introduce implicit criticism of society. The more people who read his book, the more people who were exposed to his ideas and encouraged to think about the injustices which were brought to their attention. In contrast to preaching to the converted at political rallies etc., a popular novel had the potential to reach millions of people from all walks of life, each one of whom would be exposed to the ideas of the author. "Of Mice and Men" certainly reached the wide audience which Steinbeck wanted to air his ideas.

# Discussion on why the author created each character - what did each character contribute to the message which the author wanted to put across?

Steinbeck's characters are the chief vehicles for putting his ideas across. Each character is representative of a section of the society of the time and was used to represent the influences and effects of society on that particular group of citizens. Thus, Curley's Wife can be seen to represent women and Crooks can be seen to represent the position of black people at the time.

So, let's look at the reasons why Steinbeck included certain characters in his book and what benefits they added to the messages he wanted to put across.

# What is the point of Candy?

Candy is nearing the end of his working life. Before long, he will no longer be useful to employers. He is included as an example of someone at the end of his usefulness to a money making society. Steinbeck uses Candy to comment on the way American society at the time treated people as commercial property. When Candy starts to feel he has a future through George and Lennie's dream, he becomes much more confident and assertive. *'We got our own lan', and it's ours, an we c'n go to it.'*

Candy also helps to illustrate how people can be stronger when they work together rather than individually. When Candy adds his economic strength to George and Lennie's, the dream for a while, becomes attainable.

# What is the point of Crooks?

Steinbeck created Crooks as a means to comment on and get his readers to think about racism in their society. He made Crooks intelligent and well read, expert at his job and knowledgeable about life. Through Crooks, Steinbeck's readers could see the injustice of racism when an obviously intelligent and skilful man is treated as a second class citizen who could be killed if a white person such as Curley's Wife decides to accuse him of anything.

Curley's wife emphasises the power of racism when she speaks to Crooks – '*I could get you strung up on a tree so easy it ain't even funny'*.

# What is the point of Curley?

Curley does not have to worry about money or a job as the other characters do. He has not earned his comfortable position but, as the son of the boss, he is secure. He is still very lonely and Steinbeck uses his character to show a different aspect of the theme of loneliness. Whilst most of the other characters are lonely as a result of their economic situation (having to move around), Curley is lonely because of his behaviour and unpleasant attitude. He feels that the only way he can earn respect is through aggression. Steinbeck uses the character of Curley to make his readers think about people who are in comfortable positions through no merit of their own.

# What is the point of Curley's Wife?

She has married Curley to try to escape from her previous life. She now realises that she has put herself into a worse position. She is the only woman on the ranch and is very lonely as the only person who it is acceptable to talk to is Curley. Each time she tries to talk to any of the men, she is seen as a flirt although she really just wants to talk to other people.

Curley's Wife doesn't mind who she talks to as long as she can talk to someone – she is even happy to talk to Lennie.

At the time, women were considered less important than men and it is noticeable that she is not given a name, only "Curley's Wife". This shows that she is considered to be Curley's property. She has always been in a position to be used by men as we can see from her revelations about men she has met who have promised her roles in movies and shows.

The only person who Curley's Wife can feel superior to is Crooks and she shows this when she points out that as a white woman, she could easily falsely accuse him leading to his death. In this respect, she is an effective tool of the author to exhibit the stunning injustice of the racist society of the time.

John Steinbeck wanted his readers to feel sympathy for Curley's Wife – she is a young girl who has foolishly married Curley and now finds herself trapped in a miserable life with no escape. Maybe he hoped that this would make his readers think about the position of women in 1930s America.

*Make your own notes here:*

# What is the point of Slim?

An unusual character in that he is established at the ranch, cares about others and is thoughtful and fair minded. Slim is not representative of the America which Steinbeck is criticising.

Therefore we must deduce that Slim represents something which is important to Steinbeck's message. This could be:

    a) He is the voice of the author

       OR

    b) He is the sort of person who Steinbeck wants to see making policy in America.

Slim considers situations carefully and makes decisions based upon what he thinks is best for all. This is the opposite to Steinbeck's opinion of the American Government at the time.

As a structural device to make the novel work, Slim allows George to talk and this is how we learn the past history of George and Lennie.

# What is the point of Whit?

On the surface, Whit is a very minor character but his small contribution emphasises some of Steinbeck's points about American society at the time.

Whit's fond memories of Bill Tanner, a man he had worked with for a very short time, underline the loneliness of the migrant worker. This also serves to underline the value of partnerships such as George and Lennie's.

Whit also reminds us that here is a man at the start of his working life – he could become Candy, Carlson, Slim, George depending upon how his life works out. We assume that Steinbeck wants him to turn out like Slim or George.

# What is the point of the Boss?

The Boss is the overall authority on the ranch and has the authority to "can" any of the workers whenever he likes. In "Of Mice and Men", Steinbeck could be using this character to represent the government – removed from ordinary people with the autocratic right to control their lives on a whim.

He is seen to be generally benign, not interfering as long as his ranch is running effectively. This could be representative of a government happy to let all the injustices and unfairness continue as long as its own comfort is not affected. One of the worrying aspects of the Boss's lethargy is that, after his day, Curley will step into his shoes showing that people are always at the mercy of their ruling classes.

# What is the point of the bus driver?

The bus driver at the beginning dropped George and Lennie miles out of their way because he cannot be bothered to vary his routine. Could this be representative of Steinbeck's view of the workings of society – things are done in a certain way which is not necessarily the most humane or convenient but suits the selfish needs of a minority? There is no consideration of the varied needs of individuals.

# What is the point of Carlson?

Carlson is an example of someone who has adapted to the lifestyle of the migrant worker in America at the time the novel is set. Carlson is completely insensitive to the feelings of others. We see this in the way he talks Candy into allowing him to shoot his dog. He doesn't have any understanding of the emotional pain which Candy is going through.

Through Carlson, Steinbeck is showing his audience what the life of a migrant worker could do to a man's humanity. Carlson's insensitivity is emphasised in the last line of the novel when George has just killed Lennie.

In terms of Steinbeck's message to his readers, we may assume that Carlson represents American society of the time – insensitive, selfish and unable to adapt. It is interesting to imagine what Carlson's outlook would be when he gets to Candy's age and is no longer able to control his own destiny.

Carlson utters the last words of the novel:

'Now what the hell ya suppose is eatin' them two guys?'

This shows his complete insensitivity to what has occurred and by extension could be seen to be Steinbeck's condemnation of American society's insensitivity to the plight of its workers.

*Make your own notes here:*

# What is the point of George?

George is the 'everyman' of the novel – he is trapped in a certain life but has personal values and dreams above his current position. Steinbeck wants the reader to identify with George and to put themselves in his position. George is Steinbeck's vehicle to deliver the idea of the dream which, on the surface, is to have an ideal life in a place of their own. The real meaning of the dream is to show a craving for independence and the individual's need for control over their own lives. George's vision of their own ranch represents a place where he can't be used and controlled by society but can live by his own values.

Through his relationship with Lennie, George allows Steinbeck to show that people working together can achieve far more than one individual striving for his own gain. Together, George and Lennie have more economic power and a better chance of getting out of the cycle of the migrant worker. Once Candy is allowed into the dream, the dream becomes almost achievable.

# What is the point of Lennie?

Lennie represents people who don't fit in to the accepted ideas of American society of the time. He is useful to society as a worker but cannot be fully controlled which makes him an outsider. Steinbeck uses Lennie to show how American society was unsympathetic to people with differences. Through the lack of understanding shown towards Lennie we see Steinbeck portraying a society which tries to destroy differences in order to maintain the status quo rather than celebrating and benefiting from differences.

Lennie's understanding of the dream is somewhat different to that of George. In keeping with his childlike understanding, Lennie sees their own place as a place where he can play to his heart's content, free from the restrictions and stress of the real world which he doesn't understand.

*Make your own notes here:*

# What is the point of Candy's dog?

Candy's dog's chief value to the novel is through the parallels which can be drawn. Here is a creature that has worked hard and effectively throughout his life but has now out lived his usefulness. Society's attitude to him as displayed through the character of Carlson, is to get rid of him as he can no longer produce value. There are two clear parallels here:

1. The parallel to Candy himself who has worked all his life and now that he is no longer productive, can only look forward to insecurity and being discarded.
2. The parallel to Lennie whose productivity is still high but the problems of accommodating him have become too great

In the first case, Candy will only have a comfortable old age if he can create it himself in partnership with others – society will do nothing for him.

In the second case, George takes the responsibility of releasing Lennie from a society which will make him suffer for being different.

Steinbeck in both cases shows American society in a bad light in the hope of encouraging his readers to question the morals of a society such as this.


# What is the significance of the ranch?

The ranch represents a microcosm of American society at the time. We have representatives of all levels of society as seen by Steinbeck. We have the 'ruling classes in The Boss and Curley, the 'middle manager in Slim, the workers or wealth creators and a selection of struggling minorities.

The bunkhouse – the majority of people working on the ranch live there.

The Bosses' house – the more privileged, secure and influential section of society live there.

The barn and Crooks' room – the segregation of sections of society.

The bunkhouse provides Steinbeck with a platform from which to present his interpretation of 1930s America along with his implied criticism of the society.

# What is the significance of the horseshoe game?

The horseshoe game is one area of life in the novel where all participants can compete on the same level. Thus Crooks is one of the most successful players giving the lie to the idea of any race being superior to another. Along with the card game solitaire and visits to town, it is one of the limited recreational opportunities for the workers. As a structural tool, it is the distraction which allows Lennie and Curley's Wife to be alone together in the barn leading to her death.

# What is the significance of the opening scene?

The opening scene forms a buffer between anything that has happened before and sets George and Lennie up for a new start at the ranch. However, the foreshadowing throughout the scene clearly tells us that previous problems are going to re-emerge.

The surroundings are peaceful and private and they give George and Lennie a retreat or safe place from the threats and dangers of the life they lead. They feel safe and are able to be themselves, allowing time to indulge in developing their dream.

# What is the significance of the closing scene?

In the final scene, the novel has come full circle – George and Lennie have come back to the situation of being fugitives from a society which Lennie is unable to fit in to. They are back in a safe place and George has to take the decision to release Lennie from the spiral of destruction. Arguably, Lennie actually achieves his dream as George shoots him just as he is dreaming of his beloved rabbits.

*Make your own notes here:*

# Suggestions for essay/answer planning

## Model introductions to essays on the novel

Obviously, each introduction will be different depending upon the essay question it relates to. However, it is possible to prepare general introductions which can be tweaked to link to the particular question. The model introduction below is tailored to a question about loneliness but can be adapted by changing the linking sentence at the end (the sentence "Finally...........loneliness in the novel"). If, for example, you were being asked to write about Steinbeck's criticism of American society at the time, you could change the linking sentence to the following:

*"Steinbeck uses the prevailing conditions to produce explorations of the situations of many different types of American at the time. This then allows him, through individual case studies, to highlight the faults and injustices of American society."*

'Of Mice and Men' is set during what was a time of great economic hardship for many Americans. Many people were unemployed and poverty stricken and paid work was hard to find. This situation in itself, forced many people into the lonely existence of the migrant worker; travelling alone to wherever work could be found. Others, although in apparently settled situations, were isolated by the social attitudes of the time. For example, women were expected to live and behave in a certain way due to the influence of a male dominated society. In the absence of a welfare state, older people risked losing their security as they grew older and less able to work. Finally, a person's position in society could be determined by their colour. For all of these reasons, Curley's Wife, Candy and Crooks are three characters who can help us to analyse Steinbeck's presentation of loneliness in the novel.

# Detailed sample essay plan

## Have a look at the following essay title. The essay is planned for you with a model introduction and points to raise in the body of your essay.

*"How does John Steinbeck show the effect of loneliness on three characters in 'Of Mice and Men'?"*

## Introduction:

'Of Mice and Men' is set during what was a time of great economic hardship for many Americans. Many people were unemployed and poverty stricken and paid work was hard to find. This situation in itself, forced many people into the lonely existence of the migrant worker; travelling alone to wherever work could be found. Others, although in apparently settled situations, were isolated by the social attitudes of the time. For example, women were expected to live and behave in a certain way due to the influence of a male dominated society. In the absence of a welfare state, older people risked losing their security as they grew older and less able to work. Finally, a person's position in society could be determined by their colour. For all of these reasons, Curley's Wife, Candy and Crooks are three characters who can help us to analyse Steinbeck's presentation of loneliness in the novel.

# Body of the essay:

## Write about the three characters –

### 1.   Curley's Wife:

- The only woman on the ranch
- Curley is very aggressive and possessive
- The men on the ranch are suspicious of her
- She only married Curley because she felt trapped in her previous life
- She is even more trapped now she has married Curley
- She had dreams for her future

### 2.   Candy:

- The oldest person on the ranch
- Frightened of losing his job
- His dog is his main companion
- The dog is killed as he is no longer useful
- Candy feels he has no future – as he gets older, he will no longer be useful and will lose his job
- When he has no job, he will not be able to support himself
- He wants to be a part of George and Lennie's dream

### 3.   Crooks:

- He is the only black person on the ranch
- He is not allowed into the bunkhouse because he is black
- He has his own separate room
- He is good at his job
- He would like to be a part of George and Lennie's dream

# Useful targeted quotes

*'A guy needs somebody – to be near him' (Crooks)*

*'A guy gets too lonely an' he gets sick' (Crooks)*

*'S'pose you couldn't go into the bunkhouse and play rummy 'cause you was black' (Crooks,)*

*'Aint I got a right to talk to nobody?' (Curley's Wife)*

*'I don't like Curley. He ain't a nice fella' (Curley's Wife)*

*'They'll can me purty soon' (Candy)*

*'When they can me here, I wisht somebody'd shoot me' (Candy)*

*'I won't have no place to go an' I can't get no more jobs' (Candy)*

*You seen what they done to my dog tonight' (Candy)*

*'Ranch with a bunch of guys aint no place for a girl, specially like her' (George)*

*"Come on in. If ever'body's comin' in, you might as well" It was difficult for Crooks to conceal his pleasure with anger. (Crooks)*

# Some essay titles to practice with:

Essay question:

*Why is George and Lennie's dream important in 'Of Mice and Men'?*

- What was the dream?
- What did the dream mean to Lennie?
- What did the dream mean to George?
- What did the dream mean to Candy?
- How would the dream make their lives better?

# Other questions to practice with:

- *Why are Carlson and Slim important to the novel "Of Mice and Men"?*

- *Why did George kill Lennie at the end of the novel?*

- *Why are dreams and ambitions important to the characters in "Of Mice and Men"?*

- *What would George, Lennie and Candy have gained if their dream had come true?*

- *What was John Steinbeck trying to tell the people of America through the novel "Of Mice and Men"?*

Finally, as always, it must be emphasised that this booklet is by no means a comprehensive guide to the play. The aim is to add levels of analysis to a strong foundation of understanding in order to make sure of the higher grades in your end result.

<u>Other guides in this series:</u>

"Romeo and Juliet" A* Guide from ACE Notes

"AQA Anthology 'Conflict' Section" A* Guide from ACE Notes

AQA English G.C.S.E. A* Guide from ACE Notes

"An Inspector Calls" A* Guide from ACE Notes

All currently available on Kindle and published in hard copy through Amazon.

Printed in Great Britain
by Amazon